The Rockwool Foundation Research Unit

Study Paper No. 73

Goal Prioritization and Commitment in Public Organizations

Exploring the Effects of Goal Conflict

Camilla Denager Staniok

University Press of Southern Denmark

Odense 2014

Goal Prioritization and Commitment in Public Organizations:

Exploring the Effects of Goal Conflict

Study Paper No. 73

Published by:
© The Rockwool Foundation Research Unit

Address:
The Rockwool Foundation Research Unit
Soelvgade 10, 2.tv.
DK-1307 Copenhagen K

Telephone	+45 33 34 48 00
E-mail	forskningsenheden@rff.dk
web site:	www.en.rff.dk

ISBN 978-87-93119-15-4
ISSN 0908-3979

August 2014

ABSTRACT

Public personnel policies increasingly adapt performance management systems that focus on goal attainment making *goal commitment* a critical issue in contemporary public administration research. Few studies have however empirically investigated how context factors such as goal conflicts reduce or hinder goal commitment. Accordingly, this paper investigates the interplay between public managers' goal prioritization, goal conflict and employees' goal commitment. Multilevel data from two electronic surveys of 67 principals and 1362 teachers in secondary education show that goal conflict moderates the association between principals' goal prioritization and teachers' goal commitment. More specifically, analyses show that there is no independent significant association between principals' goal prioritization and teachers' goal commitment, but that goal conflict has a significant negative effect on this relationship. The results thus suggest that goal conflict is an important context factor connected to the relationship between managers' goal prioritization and employees' goal commitment. On that background this study more generally adds to our knowledge about the *conditions* for reciprocal effects between managers and employees in a public context.

Keywords. Goal commitment, goal prioritization, goal conflict, public organizations, management

INTRODUCTION

Several studies of goal setting in public organizations support that *goal commitment* is important for goals to have performance implications (e.g. Locke & Latham, 1990; Klein et al., 1999). Latham, Borgogni and Petitta for an example describe commitment as the "sine qua none" of goal attainment (Latham et al., 2008). Most studies, however, only investigate how goal commitment moderates the effects of goal setting on organizational performance (Locke & Latham, 2002; Perry et al., 2006). Surprisingly few studies empirically investigate the link between public management and employees' goal commitment as well as the impact of context factors such as goal conflict. The question of goal commitment is important in its own right, because public personnel policies increasingly adapt performance management systems that focus on goal attainment, but also because it helps us to understand, how public employees can be motivated to perform the duties and responsibilities assigned by the organization and society. A crucial question left unanswered is thus whether there is an association between public management and employees' goal commitment and how goal conflict affects this relationship?

In this paper the association between public management and employees' goal commitment is explored by investigating the reciprocal effects of managers' prioritization of a goal and employees' goal commitment. The theoretical expectations are twofold. On one hand managers' prioritization of a goal is expected to challenge, encourage and inspire employees to assume greater ownership of their work attitudes and thus increase employees' commitment to the goal (Wright, 2007; Perry et al. 2006; Locke et al., 1994). On the other hand, employees' goal commitment is expected to affect managers' prioritization of a goal, because managers' in order to deal with a low goal commitment among employees can be expected to increase their prioritization of this goal.

However, as public organizations most often are funded by individuals, who do not receive the direct benefit of the goods or services the organizations produce, there are simultaneous demands for equity, accountability, and responsiveness, in addition to demands for economic efficiency (Wilson, 1989; Rainey, 2009; Wright, 2004). As a result employees of public organizations are often confronted with multiple and even conflicting goals. In other words, the context of public organizations counts when it comes to goals. As noted by Wright though: "given the purported importance of the work context for work motivation in the public sector, there has been surprisingly little empirical investigation of this relationship" (Wright, 2001: 573-574). Furthermore Locke and colleagues argue that "although commitment to any given goal should be reduced by goal conflict, there had been no studies which focused on intra-individual conflict within the goal setting paradigm" (Locke et al., 1994: 67). Intra-individual goal conflicts are here defined as employee-perceived goal conflicts that involve different types of goals on a single task (Locke et al., 1994). Accordingly, intra-individual goal conflict is included in this study and expected to have a negative effect on both employees' goal commitment and the relationship between managers' goal prioritization and employees' goal commitment. More concrete, *employees* are expected to be less receptive to managers' goal prioritization because they would feel that it entailed incompatible action tendencies (Locke et al., 1994), and *managers* less likely to prioritize a goal if he or she knows that employees perceive a conflict between this goal and another goal. Because the relationship between managers' goal prioritization, employees' goal commitment and goal conflict is ambiguous discussions throughout the paper will return to the issue of whether and how the concepts are related and/or interdependent.

The relationship between managers' goal prioritization, employees' goal commitment and goal conflict is investigated empirically in the area of secondary education in Denmark. This is a well-suited area, because employees refer to one manager in well-defined organizations that face two prevalent and potentially conflicting goals: a high level of completion and a high academic level. Recent national reforms of restructuring have transformed the financial system of the area from spending caps to activity-based budgeting, which have increased the economic incentives and competition among the schools. On one hand reforms thus raise demands on teachers for securing a high level of completion in order to secure school finances, which could imply lowering the academic level. On the other hand the teachers can be characterized as a semi-profession with strong professional norms (Freidson, 2001; Roberts and Dietrich, 1999), which can be expected to raise demands on teachers for striving towards the highest academic level. In continuation hereof, the area of secondary education in Denmark also constitutes a *hard test*. The area is extremely institutionalized with both strong professional norms and collective agreements, which can be expected to complicate or even obstruct managerial influence on employees' work attitudes. Moreover there is substantial variation in teachers' perceptions of the two goals as well as in principals' goal prioritization.

Data from two electronic surveys of 67 principals and 1362 teachers provides an unusual opportunity to study the relationship of goal commitment and goal conflict in a multi-level setup at both manager and employee level. The rich dataset furthermore enables control for an array of teacher characteristics and unobserved institutional factors such as principal-, school- and municipal characteristics, which could potentially influence teachers' goal commitment. Thus, this study contributes to the vast literature on goal commitment in public organizations by proposing and testing the effects of goal conflict on a unique dataset.

In the next section the theoretical expectations and main hypotheses are described. This is followed by an outline of the study's research design, data and methods. Finally, the results are presented, and a concluding discussion comments on limitations of the study and suggests avenues for future research.

DEFINING GOAL COMMITMENT: A VALUE ORIENTED APPROACH

What does goal commitment mean? According to Meyer & Allen goal commitment can be defined as "an internal force that binds an individual to a goal" (Meyer & Allen, 1997). The internal force is here interpreted as the acceptance and persistence of an individual's goal-related behavior, and in other words tells us something about an individual's determination to reach a goal (Wright, 2007). Goal commitment can be experienced differently or rely on different motives, and commitment is therefore often also argued to be a multidimensional construct (Meyer & Allan, 1993; Meyer & Herscovitch, 2001). Some individuals are committed to reach a goal because they *want* to attain the goal. They identify or feel a desire to reach the goal. Others feel they ought to attain the goal, and are thus motivated by obligations or normative considerations. Yet others feel that they have to attain the goal, in that the cost of not doing so would be too high. These different motives Meyer and Allen (1993, 1997) capture and conceptualize in a three-component model consisting of three commitment dimensions: affective commitment, normative commitment and continuance commitment respectively. The dimensions refer to the different *motives* of commitment and not to different types of commitment. This study partly relies on their conceptualization, but solely focuses on *affective commitment* and *normative commitment* for two reasons. First of all, the primary interest of this paper is to assess goal commitment empirically and previous studies have proved that affective and normative commitment are most strongly related to organizational issues and managerial attitudes compared to e.g. continuance commitment (see e.g. the meta-analysis by Meyer et al., 2002). In continuation hereof public administration scholars have argued that economic benefits associated with public sector employment are more frequently determined by external political institutions, collective agreements and economic cycles than by the internal actions of public organizations, thereby making it more difficult to adequately assess economic and exchange-oriented commitment such as continuance commitment (Stazyk et al., 2011).

Secondly, affective commitment and normative commitment are closely related dimensions compared to continuance commitment in that they both rely on the *values* of the individual. Early assessments of Meyer and Allen's three-component model suggested that each dimension should be included when evaluating employee commitment (Dunham et al., 1994; Hackett et al., 1994; Meyer et al., 1993). However, a later extensive meta-analysis of studies using the three-component model by Meyer and colleagues themselves concluded that affective and normative commitment is often highly correlated and that results regarding continuance commitment vary considerably (Meyer et al., 2002). In some studies continuance commitment has even been shown to have the opposite effect on organizational issues and employee-related behavior than normative and affective commitment (Hackett et al., 1994; Meyer et al., 1993; Dunham et al., 1994).

On that background this study thus takes an approach that *partly* resembles what Angle and Perry (1981) early on denoted *value commitment*. Angle and Perry describes value commitment as an individual's support of the goals of the organization (Angle & Perry; 1981: 4), where support is understood more concretely as a sense of "pride in association with the organization (i.e., identification), willingness to perform for the organization, concern for the fate of the organization, and congruence of personal values with those of the organization" (Angle & Perry, 1981: 4). Accordingly, normative goal commitment and affective goal commitment is here argued to describe individuals' support for the values inherent in a goal, their identification with the goal, their feelings of obligations to perform in order to reach the goal, and their concern for the fate of the goal. The value-oriented approach to goal commitment applied here compared to that of Angle and Perry, however, differs in two important respects. First of all, it focuses only on commitment to a specific performance goal and not a sum of organizational goals. Secondly, it treats congruence of personal values and those of the organization as distinct form goal commitment and instead as an expression of goal conflict. Figure 1 below illustrates this paper's value oriented approach to goal commitment.

Figure 1. Illustration of the value oriented approach to goal commitment

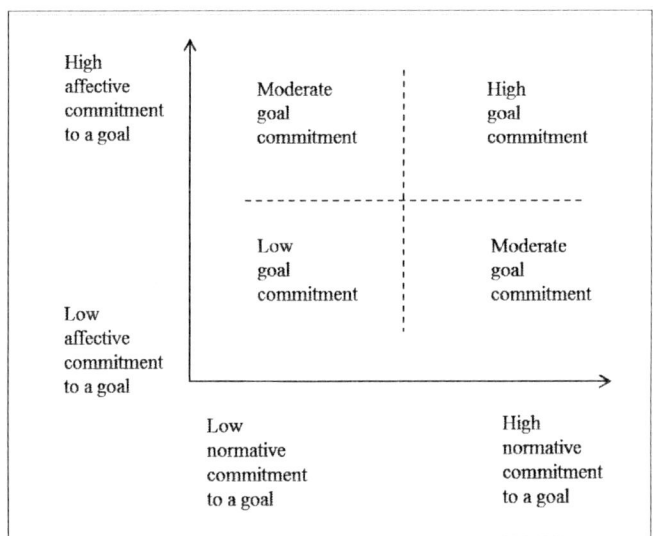

Summing up, employees with a high goal commitment thus strive to achieve a goal because they *want* to *and* feel they *ought* to (Meyer et al., 1993). In the following, the theoretical expectations about the association between managers' goal prioritization, goal conflict and employees' goal commitment will be discussed. Based on this, four empirically testable hypotheses about the relationships will be proposed.

GOAL PRIORITIZATION AND GOAL COMMITMENT:
THEORETICAL EXPECTATIONS

What is the relationship between public managers' goal prioritization and employees' commitment to a goal? The immense literature on goal setting offers several suggestions on how public managers can affect employees' goal commitment. Broadly speaking one can distinguish between managerial efforts directed towards: 1) the process of designing the goals and the characteristics of the goal (e.g. Locke & Latham, 2002), 2) monetary incentives and feedback (e.g. Klein et al., 1999), and 3) prioritizing and communication of goals (e.g. Wright, 2001). To date, limited application of goal-setting theory exists in empirical research on employee motivation in public settings and empirical knowledge is thus needed in all three matters (Perry et al., 2006). This study, however, focus exclusively on the latter as it approaches the effects of managers' goal prioritization. The next section discusses the most relevant and recent contributions in this more specific stream of research.

With reference to goal setting theory and its more than 40 years of research history this study builds on the underlying assumption that conscious and well-specified goals affect the actions and attitudes of employees (Latham et al., 2008). Goals are here defined as "the object or aim of an action to attain a particular standard of performance" (Perry et al. 2006: 509). In order to propose testable hypothesis of the relationship between goal prioritization and goal commitment it is necessary to assess the mechanisms of how commitment develops.

Meyer and Herscovitch (2001) propose that any personal or situational variable that contribute to the likelihood that an individual becomes involved in a goal, recognizes the value-relevance of association with a goal, and/or derive his of her identity from working towards an objective will contribute to the development of affective goal commitment. Moreover, normative commitment is argued to develop when an individual has internalized a set of norms concerning appropriate conduct (i.e. through socialization), and/or is the recipient of benefits *and* experiences a need to reciprocate (Meyer & Herscovitch, 2001: 316-317). Meyer, Allen and Topolnytsky have also suggested that normative commitment might reflect an individual's recognition of his or her feelings of obligation as part of the individual's "psychological contract" (Rousseau, 1989) with the organization (Meyer et al., 1998).

The discussion section will return to this point, as individuals might experience diverse obligations as part of other "psychological contracts" as well, which may very well also affect their commitment to a given goal. On this background goal commitment develops when an employee feels personally related to or responsible for achieving a goal, and thus suggests that public managers should strive to increase employees' feeling of connectedness and responsibility to the organization and the goals.

In similar vein, Wright (2007) argues, drawing on e.g. goal setting theory generally, but also empirical studies of Rainey and Steinbauer (1999), that employees will expend greater effort toward achieving goals they believe will result in important outcomes. Congruence between an individual's own values and the values of the goals is suggested to make individuals more likely to incorporate the goals into their own sense of identity and view their assigned roles in achieving those goals as personally meaningful. In continuation hereof Wright suggests that in order to ensure that employees are working on organizational tasks as a way to validate their self-concept, managers must emphasize not only that the organization's values coincide with those of employees, but also that employee performance contributes to the organization's ability to operationalize those values: "managers can inspire their employees to work harder by clearly communicating how their work benefits society" (Wright, 2007: 60).

Research on goal commitment and goal setting more generally thus indicate that the key to affect employees' goal commitment is to clearly prioritize goals and communicate their values and implications to their employees. A strong goal prioritization can in this light be expected to challenge, encourage and/or inspire employees to assume greater ownership of their work attitudes and thus increase their commitment to the goal (Wright, 2004). By prioritizing a goal managers are expected to be able to communicate the salience of the goal for the organization as a whole, signal their own commitment to reach the goal and make it easier for the employees to understand the relationship between effort and resulting performance (Porter et al, 1976; Wright, 2004). The direction of causality may however also be the other way around, as it is also very likely that managers could be influenced by the goal commitment of their employees. Few scholars have investigated or theorized about these potential effects, but it is arguable that employees' goal commitment could work as an indicator for managers in regard to where managerial effort and prioritization is needed. The expectation here is that if employees express low commitment to a specific performance goal managers will increase their priority of this goal in order to signal the importance of the goal, and thus in turn increase employees' commitment to the goal. Similarly, it could be expected that managers who see a high commitment to a specific performance goal among their employees feel no need to use valuable time, energy or effort on prioritizing this goals, and on this background lower their priority of the goal. The first expectations to be tested in this study are thus:

> *H1a: Public managers' goal prioritizing has a positive effect on employees' goal commitment*
>
> *H1b: Employees' goal commitment has a negative effect on public managers' goal prioritizing*

This hypothesized association between managers' goal prioritization and employees' goal commitment in public organizations may, however depend on the level of goal conflict. As noted by numerous scholars over time the public sector is characterized by multiple and often conflicting goals, meant to consider and satisfy different democratic and public issues of society (Wilson, 1989; Rainey, 2009). But, although goal commitment, goal setting processes and goal prioritization have been discussed extensively by public management scholars and political scientists, there have been few attempts to link them with the constructs of goal commitment and conflict. Goal conflict in the public sector often reflects that organizations are judged according to two standards that are often at odds: responsiveness to public needs and competence in the performance of tasks (Meier, 1987:112). These performance criteria and goals, combined with public expectations that public organizations meet both sets of goals, can be a source of goal ambiguity or goal conflict (Panday & Wright, 2006).

Goal conflict is however an ambiguous term in itself, in that it can refer to both inter-individual as well as intra-individual perceived conflicts (Locke et al., 1994). On one hand *inter-individual conflicts* imply conflicts between for example managers, employees, departments and coalitions or groups of organizational members. These types of conflicts have often been investigated (see e.g. Katz & Kahn, 1968; Cyert & March, 1963 and Mintzberg, 1983). On the other hand *intra-individual conflicts* according to Locke and colleagues imply that a single employee perceive a conflict either between different types of goals or different goals related to one or more tasks. They categorize intra-individual conflicts as: 1) employee perceived goal conflicts that involve divergent personal goals and assigned goals, 2) employee perceived goal conflicts that involve which of a number of different task to emphasize when multiple goals or task exist, and 3) employee perceived goal conflicts that involve different types of goals on a single task (Locke et al., 1994). Intra-individual conflicts have been not yet been studied much, but the few existing studies find, that intra-individual conflicts primarily have a negative impact on commitment and or performance (see Locke et al., (1994) for a more detailed overview).

This study focuses on the third type of intra-individual conflict in that it investigates employees' perception of a conflict between two different goals pertaining to the same task. This type of intra-individual conflict is particular interesting as public employees are very often confronted with two types of goals - "meet quantity criteria" and "meet quality criteria" - and thus potentially conflicts of which performance dimension to emphasize when completing a task (Locke et al., 1994). This type of goal conflict also mirrors what Meier denotes responsiveness to public needs and competence in the performance of tasks, respectively. Inspired by these studies goal conflict may expectedly be related to public employees' goal commitment in two ways. First of all, employees who perceive a goal conflict will be less committed to the goal because they would feel that striving toward one goal would be at the expense of another (Latham et al., 2008), and it is thus likely that conflict will have a negative effect on employees' goal commitment. This leads to the following hypothesis:

H2a: Goal conflict has a negative effect on employees' goal commitment

Secondly, employees that perceive a goal conflict will be less receptive to managers' goal prioritization, because they would feel that it entailed incompatible action tendencies (Locke et al., 1994). On this background goal conflict can also be expected to have a negative effect on the association between public managers' goal prioritization on employees' goal commitment. The final hypothesis is thus:

*H2b: Goal conflict has a negative effect on the relationship between public mangers'
goal prioritization and employees' goal commitment*

Locke and colleagues in their study of intra-individual conflicts among college professors investigate how the goals of teaching and doing research coincide for college professors and in turn affect their performance. They find that the main source of conflict was externally induced pressures from e.g. rewards systems (Locke et al., 1994). There is thus furthermore reason to expect that intra-individual conflicts will be strongest in the cases where quality and quantity criteria are also supported by economic incentives at the organizational level.

Moreover, in the light of the *sociology of professions* professional norms can be a strong determinant of employees' attitudes. Strong professions have a high-specialized theoretical knowledge, a strong client-orientation and broadly shared values and behavioral norms (Freidson, 2001; Roberts and Dietrich, 1999), which could increase employees' perceptions of goal conflicts. The strong norms of a profession can be expected to constitute potentially competing values that challenge principals' in influencing their teachers' goal commitment. A clash between professional norms and managers' goal prioritization may arise because both depend on whether the teacher recognizes the value-relevance of and/or derives his or her identity from the profession or the inherent values of the goals (Meyer et al., 2001). It is therefore also expectable that intra-individual conflicts will be strongest in the cases where public employees have strong rather than weak professional norms. The paper will return to these issues in both the methodological sections below as well as in the final discussion. Concluding, figure 2 below depicts the theoretical expectations and hypotheses of the paper.

Figure 2. Theoretical expectations and hypotheses

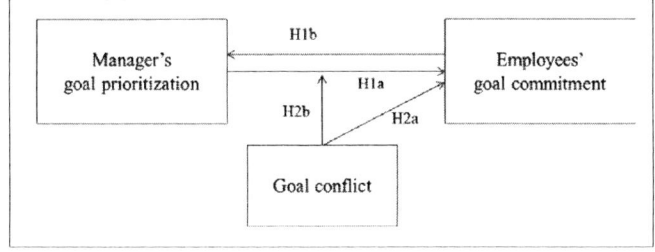

REASERCH DESIGN

This study investigates the relationship between managers' goal prioritization, goal conflict and employees' goal commitment empirically in the area of secondary education in Denmark. The study focuses on the largest type of general education; STX schools. STX schools provide general education to almost half of the Danish Youth (around 42.000 students in 2010 according to The Ministry of Children and Education, 2010), and all STX schools are nationally regulated and tuition free. The area is well-suited for three reasons. First of all, schools in this area are similar both in regard to the services they produce and the internal management structures of the organizations. Nearly all principals engage with teachers on a daily basis and can in most cases be said to personify the management of the schools. Almost all principals also handle the personnel management of the teachers, which both implies that all teachers refer to the same manager and that there is good reason to expect that principals will be able to influence the teachers.

Secondly, due to recent reforms of restructuring the financial system has been transformed from spending caps to activity-based budgeting (based on the number of students enrolled and passing exams), and considerable decision-making authority has therefore been decentralized from the Ministry of Education and the counties to the principals. Schools are now self-governing with school boards responsible for the overall direction of the schools. The reforms have thus increased autonomy and the demand for strategic leadership within the schools as well as made substantial room for goal prioritization at the school level.

Furthermore, partly due to the reforms, the schools now face two prevalent and potentially conflicting goals: a high level of completion and a high academic level. Activity-based budgeting has increased the economic incentives and competition among the schools. On one hand the reforms have thus raised demands on teachers for securing a high level of completion in order to secure school finances, which could imply lowering the academic level. On the other hand the teachers in upper secondary education can be described as a semi-profession with rather strong professional norms (Freidson, 2001; Roberts and Dietrich, 1999) inducing them to strive towards the highest possible academic level.

DATA

The data for this study was collected in November-December 2012 and consist of two parallel surveys to both principals and teachers at STX schools in Denmark. 135 STX schools were invited to participate. In October 2012 letters to the schools requesting contact information for all principals and teachers were sent. Most schools gave the information, and for most other schools, information was available on their websites. Nine schools were left out of the investigation either because they actively refused to participate, or because we could not obtain contact information to all teachers. In late November, web-based questionnaires to 135 principals and 8,600 teachers were sent out, and throughout December additionally four reminders to those, who had not yet responded followed. When the survey was closed on December 21st, 76 principals and 2,934 teachers (response rates 60.3 percent and 34.1 percent respectively) had completed the survey. 67 principal responses were complete, and these along with the 1,362 teachers at the schools are used in the analyses below. The teacher dataset has been merged with the principal dataset allowing a multilevel analysis.

MEASURES

The main variables in the dataset are commitment and leadership items, which are measured among both teachers and principals. All items were translated into English and back again to validate the content of the items. Before the actual survey a pilot study to 150 teachers and one principal was conducted and this resulted in several significant adjustments of the survey. Primarily, the survey was shortened, but also the wording of some items was changed.

The dependent variable, goal commitment, is operationalized as teachers' commitment to the goal of a high completion rate and measured with four items, which reflect both affective and normative commitment (all items have a positive wording - see also Appendix A, Table A1). The items are taken from an article of Meyer & Herscovitch (2001: 320), which conceptualizes and distinguishes between different *types* of commitment in the workplace (e.g. goal commitment, organizational commitment and commitment to change). Their scale on *goal commitment* is rather new, but the corresponding dimensions and scales of their concept of organizational commitment is commonly used and highly validated (se e.g. meta-study by Meyer et al., 2002). As can be seen from Table 1 almost all the factor loadings are highly satisfactory with loadings near 0.8 and so is the scale reliability with a Cronbach's alpha at 0.85 (only one item is slightly below the recommended 0.7). It is thus reasonable to expect that all items reflect the same latent variable, goal commitment, and it furthermore supports the theoretical conceptualization of affective and normative commitment as one expression of an individual's commitment to a goal[1].

Table 1. Principal axis factoring analysis of goal commitment (oblimin rotated)

	Mean	Std. Dev.	Factor score	Cronbach's alpha
Commitment to the goal of a high completion rate	59.26	22.41		0.85
"Achieving a high completion rate is as important to me as it is to the school" (affective1)	2.98	1.21	0.74	
"I really want to achieve a high completion rate" (affective2)	3.59	1.05	0,79	
"I feel obliged to do my best to achieve a high completion rate" (normative1)	3.63	1.03	0,77	
"I owe it to my school to do my best to achieve a high completion rate" (normative2)	3.29	1.09	0,69	

The *main independent variable*, goal prioritization, is measured by asking the principals how they prioritize the goal of a high completion rate on a scale from 1 to 7 compared to six other relevant goals (1=highest priority and 7=lowest priority – see also Appendix A, Table 1A). Principals were forced to rank the goals differently as the same number could only be assigned once, but they were able to skip the question or write 0. 0 was coded as not prioritizing the goal. The item has afterwards been reversed, so 7 correspond to a high priority and 1 to a low priority. No principals answered 0.

Next, *the moderating variable*, goal conflict, is measured by a single item asking teachers to what degree (scale from 0-10) they experience a conflict between achieving a high academic level and a high completion rate. 10 was coded as "to a very high degree" and 0 as "not at all" (see also Appen-

---

[1] A principal axis factoring analysis including all three dimensions confirmed the expectations that continuance commitment varied markedly from the two other dimensions.

dix A, Table 1A). The goals of achieving a high completion rate and a high academic level are two different and potentially conflicting goals pertaining to the same task - teaching - and thus used to measure intra-individual goal conflict. Achieving a high completion rate contrasts with the goal of achieving a high academic level in that a high commitment to completion might induce teachers to lower the academic level in order to make sure that all students are able to keep up with the teaching and in the end complete their education. The two types of goals represent typical quality versus quantity performance criteria that entail incompatible action tendencies. They are furthermore, as mentioned above, supported by economic and strategic incentives on the organizational level on one hand and professional norms on the other.

Finally several *control variables*, at both teacher and school level, was included in the analyses. Table 1 shows the summary statistics of both explanatory and control variables, which are mainly self-reported in the survey, including age, gender, and tenure (general and organizational). From the teacher survey, we have gathered information on the teachers' subjects, which have been coded into broad areas (science or non-science). The number of teachers is gathered from our lists of respondents, which cover all teachers at each school.

Table 2. Sample characteristics ($n_{principals} = 67$, $n_{teachers} = 1.298$)

	Mean	Std.Dev.	Min.	Max.
School level				
Principals' goal prioritization	3.249433	1.465097	1	7
Principal age	57.92	6.53	42	69
Principal gender (female=1)	0.26	0.44	0	1
Principal tenure (years, current school)	11.52	7.53	0	31
School size (number of teachers)	81.08	20.02	38	137
Teacher level				
Teachers' goal commitment	59.26	22.41	1	7
Goal conflict	6.35	2.70	0	10
Age	44.84	11.52	24	71
Gender (female=1)	0.52	0.50	0	1
Tenure (years, current school)	11.50	11.05	0	48
Teaching area (science=1)	0.25	0.44	0	1
Part time	0.19	0.39	0	1

Non-science teachers and *female* teachers are expected to be more affectively committed to a high completion rate as they expectedly are more emotional and therefore potentially more concerned about including all the students and making sure that everyone can keep up with the academic level. Also it is expected that *part-time* teachers are less committed to the goal of a high completion rate than full-time teachers, at least in the situations where they have other obligations and or /a job in another organization. However, it is not unthinkable that part-time employees will be more goal committed than full-time employees, if they are striving towards a getting a full-time position. Even though there is no clear conceptual basis for the impact of *age* and *tenure* on goal commitment (Klein et al., 1999) older teachers and teachers with a high tenure at the school are in this context expected to be less committed to the goal of a high completion rate, because they are expected to be more independent with their own professional agendas and thus less sensitive to managerial prioritizations and raised demands for ensuring a high completion rate.

Furthermore, a number of school level characteristics related to both the school and the principal can be important for goal prioritization and goal commitment. Regarding leader characteristics gender, age and tenure in the current position are included as control variables. The literature offers few findings on these aspects, so they are included mainly for control purposes. The analyses also control for school size (number of teachers), and commitment to the goal of a high completion rate is expected to be negatively related to organization size. Smaller schools also represent smaller communities where it is expectable that individual considerations and feelings of social responsibility towards all students would be more prevailing. Correlations and item wordings regarding all variables can be seen in the Appendix A, Table A1-2.

METHODS

The analysis of how managers' goal prioritization and goal conflict affect employees' goal commitment is performed as a series of random effects models where the relevant control variables and the independent variables have been included stepwise. A fixed effect model would not be applicable as the main independent variable (managers' goal prioritization) only varies at the organizational level. Instead the random effects models include controls for all relevant individual characteristics that could potentially affect principals' goal prioritization as mentioned above. To investigate the moderating effect of goal conflict on the relationship between managers' goal prioritization and employees' goal commitment an interaction term (goal prioritization x goal conflict) has been created and added to the final model. If the interaction term is statistically significant, we have an indication that the effect of principals' goal prioritization on teachers' goal commitment depends on teachers' perception of goal conflict.

RESULTS

Table 3 (see page 20) provides the multilevel regression analysis of the influence of principals' goal prioritization and teacher perceived goal conflict on teachers' goal commitment. Hypothesis 1a expected a positive association between principals' prioritization of the goal of achieving a high completion rate and teachers' commitment to the same goal, whereas Hypothesis 1b expected a negative association. Model 2 shows that neither expectation can be confirmed and Hypotheses 1a and b are therefore rejected. Controlled for a number of relevant variables such as teacher and principal age, gender and tenure, the degree to which principals' prioritize the goal of a high completion rate does not have a significant association with teachers' commitment to the goal.

As we move to Model 3, which introduces the variable measuring to which degree teachers perceive a goal conflict between achieving a high academic level and a high completion rate, we see, as expected from Hypothesis 2a, that perceiving goal conflict is strongly negatively associated with teachers' commitment to the goal of achieving a high completion rate. Hypothesis 2a is thus confirmed.

Model 4 shows that teachers' perception of goal conflict furthermore *moderates* the effect of principals' goal prioritization on teachers' goal commitment. From Hypotheses 2b it was expected that goal conflict would have a negative effect on the relationship between principals' goal prioritization and teachers' goal commitment. The statistically significant and negative interaction term between principals' goal prioritization and teachers' perception of goal conflict confirms this expectation. This result tells us that the effect of principals' prioritization of the goal of a high completion rate on teachers' commitment to the same goal differ according to whether teachers perceive a conflict between achieving a high academic level and a high completion rate. The result is depicted in figure 3 below.

Figure 3. Illustration of estimated differences in marginal effects dependent on the level of teacher perceived goal conflict

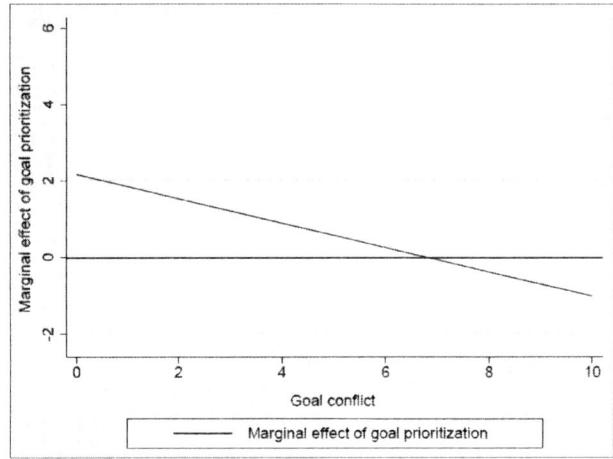

Figure 3 illustrates the significant difference of marginal effects as dependent on the level of goal conflict, and shows that the estimates becomes negative when goal conflict surpasses 6.8 (on the scale from 0-10). Note though, that in this case the marginal effects of principals' goal prioritization on teachers' goal commitment are not significant, however the slope of line, which illustrates the marginal effects of principals goal prioritization, is significantly different from 0. This tells us, in accordance with the results of Model 4, that our best estimate of the association between principals' goal prioritization and teachers' goal commitment depends on teachers' perception of goal conflict.

Finally, regarding the relationship between a range of different control variables and teachers' goal commitment, Table 3 shows that none of the school level control variables are significantly associated with teachers' goal commitment whereas several of the teacher level control variables are (gender and part time are the exceptions). More specifically we see that older teachers are significantly more committed to the goal of achieving a high completion rate than younger teachers, but that tenure is significant negatively related to teachers' goal commitment. Furthermore science teachers have a significant and markedly lower goal commitment than teachers in other areas. The main findings are now discussed in the light of the theoretical expectations and previous research.

Table 3. Multilevel regression of employees' goal commitment (random effects, unstandardized regression, t stats in parentheses)

	Model 1	Model 2	Model 3	Model 4
Teacher level control variables				
Age (years)	0.405***	0.405***	0.323***	0.323***
	(4.31)	(4.31)	(3.57)	(3.59)
Gender (female=1)	1.885	1.884	1.936*	1.862
	(1.75)	(1.75)	(2.01)	(1.93)
Tenure, current job (years)	-0.311**	-0.311**	-0.281**	-0.278**
	(-3.14)	(-3.14)	(-2.93)	(-2.93)
Teaching area (science=1, other =0)	-3.887**	-3.889**	-3.652**	-3.595**
	(-2.73)	(-2.73)	(-2.75)	(-2.71)
Part time	0.914	0.909	0.905	0.986
	(0.68)	(0.67)	(0.68)	(0.74)
School level control variables				
Principal age (years)	0.215	0.215	0.170	0.184
	(1.38)	(1.40)	(1.03)	(1.13)
Principal gender (female=1)	1.266	1.257	0.496	0.534
	(0.67)	(0.66)	(0.28)	(0.30)
Principal tenure, current job (years)	-0.124	-0.124	-0.135	-0.131
	(-0.93)	(-0.93)	(-0.97)	(-0.96)
School size (no. of teachers)	-0.0476	-0.0478	-0.0517	-0.0597
	(-1.15)	(-1.15)	(-1.42)	(-1.69)
Principal goal prioritization		0.0244	0.171	2.165
		(0.05)	(0.31)	(1.77)
Goal conflict			-2.733***	-1.703**
			(-11.18)	(-2.89)
Goal prioritization x goal conflict				-0.318*
				(-2.07)
Constant	36.95***	36.94***	60.21***	53.51***
	(4.33)	(4.32)	(7.42)	(5.94)
n Observations (teachers)	1362	1362	1362	1362
Groups (principals)	67	67	67	67
R^2 Within	0.0217	0.0217	0.1326	0.1343
Between	0.1073	0.1071	0.0818	0.1022
Overall	0.0269	0.0269	0.1281	0.1322

* $p < 0.05$, ** $p < 0.01$, *** $p < 0.001$

DISCUSSION AND CONLUSION

The purpose of this paper has been to examine the association between management and employees' goal commitment in public organizations and to explore the effects of goal conflict. More specifically, the aim has been to begin to disentangle the interplay between managers' goal prioritization, intra-individual goal conflict and employees' goal commitment. Using multilevel survey data from Danish principals and teachers in the area of upper secondary education, two out the four hypotheses set forward are supported. The main result of the analyses is that whether teachers perceive a goal conflict is important for their goal commitment as well as for the association between principals' goal prioritization and teachers' goal commitment.

According to the results the principal's goal prioritization is not directly significantly associated with employees' goal commitment, so Hypotheses 1a and 1b are rejected. However, teachers' perception of goal conflict is significantly negatively associated with teachers' goal commitment, which confirms Hypothesis 2a. Moreover, the interaction term between principals' goal prioritization and teachers' perception of goal conflict reveals that the association between principals' goal prioritization and teachers' goal commitment depends on the extent to which teachers perceive a goal conflict. Teachers' perception of goal conflict has a statistically significant negative effect on the relationship between principals' goal prioritization and teachers' goal commitment. This finding thus lends support to Hypothesis 2b.

Regarding the rejection of Hypotheses 1a and 1b, this finding theoretically contradicts the initial expectations. Principals' prioritization of a high completion rate was expected to affect the teachers' commitment to the goal of a high completion rate positively, and teachers' commitment to a high completion rate was expected to affect the principals' prioritization of a high completion rate negatively. However, results show that this is not the case. Similar results have been found in previous studies. For an example Paarlberg and Perry (2007) find in their comparative case study that the goals communicated by the organization have little meaning for the employees' daily work, and that few employees find the communication of goals engaging and meaningful. Paarlberg and Perry's study furthermore calls attention to a variable that have not been investigated in this study, but expectedly could be important for the effect of goal prioritization, namely *how* the manager communicates the prioritization.

The reason for the rejection of hypothesis 1 in this context could also be related to the specific case of this study. Secondary education can as mentioned earlier be considered a hard test partly because teachers in upper secondary education can be described as a semi-profession. The strong norms of the profession can be expected to constitute strong competing values that challenge principals in influencing their teachers' goal commitment. At least in the cases where the prioritized values or goals contradict the teachers' professional norms, it is arguable that it would be more difficult – if not impossible – for principals to affect the teachers' goal commitment. In other words, teachers in secondary education may experience obligations as part of a "psychological contract" with a strong profession that may undermine the goal prioritization of the principal, if the goals of the profession and the goals of the principal do not coincide. In this paper the professional norms of secondary education teachers have primarily been discussed in regard to why teachers might experience a conflict between the goals of a high academic level and a high completion rate, but the failure to confirm Hypotheses 1a and 1b calls for further studies explicitly taking into consideration also the impact of professional norms for the relationship between managers' goal prioritization and employees' goal commitment.

A third alternative explanation could be found in the characteristics of the goal of achieving a high completion rate as being either to complex or to performance oriented. Previous studies within goal setting theory suggest that task *complexity* is a moderator of goal effects: "as the complexity of the task increases and higher level skills and strategies have yet to become automatized, goal effects are dependent on the ability to discover appropriate task strategies" (Locke & Latham, 2002: 708-709). Accordingly, because people vary greatly in their ability to do this, the effect size for goal setting is smaller on complex than on simple tasks (2002). Likewise, Winters and Latham find that the impact of goal complexity again depends on the *type* of goal. If a learning goal rather than a performance goal was set, high goals led to significantly higher performance on a complex task than did the general goal of urging people do their best (Winters & Latham, 1996). Most studies of this kind focus on performance and not commitment. Similar effects are, however, expectable for commitment, because employees' belief that they can attain the goal (self-efficacy) can be argued to be a key facilitator of goal commitment (Locke and Latham, 2002). Klein, Wesson, Hollenbeck and Alge (1999) for an example argue that commitment is most important and relevant when goals are difficult, and according to Locke and Latham this is because goals that are difficult for people require high effort and are associated with lower chances of success than easy goals (Locke and Latham, 2002; Erez & Zidon, 1984). Similar studies of the interplay between goal prioritization, conflict and commitment that compare different types of goals or goals pertaining to tasks of different complexity are thus relevant.

In accordance with the theoretical expectations, the analyses confirm that goal conflict has a negative impact on teachers' goal commitment, but also on the relationship between principals' goal prioritization and teachers' goal commitment. These results support similar findings within several streams of research. Empirical goal setting-studies have investigated the effects of personal versus assigned goals. Both Erez et al. (1985), Locke et al. (1988) and Vance and Colella (1990) found that discrepancy reduced commitment for the assigned goal. Also studies of value congruence in the workplace have found that congruence between individual and organizational values is positively related to positive work attitudes, including employee satisfaction, commitment, and involvement (Meglino & Ravlin, 1998). Paarlberg and Perry (2007) likewise find that strategic values are motivating employees to the extent that they reflect employees' internal affective, normative, and task-oriented values. However, the support for Hypothesis 2a and 2b also contradicts some previous findings. Locke et al. (1994) for an example do not find that intra-individual goal conflict has any significant impact on commitment as goal conflict in their study is found only to influence performance. Common for most of the mentioned studies is though, that either they 1) do not measure goal conflict directly, 2) are conducted in experimental settings, and/or 3) focus on the effects of goal conflict on performance and not commitment. The basis of comparison is thus challenged and further exploration of the interplay between goal prioritization, conflict and commitment is clearly still warranted.

In this study the association between managers' goal prioritization and employees' goal commitment have been studied as a dual causal relationship. Even though the theoretical and empirical foundation for the expectation of positive effects of the managers' goal prioritization on employees' goal commitment is most strongly supported in previous literature, the expectation that employees' goal commitment will affect managers' goal prioritization is still highly valid and reasonable – especially in the present case. Managers as well as employees are affected by their surroundings, and managers in STX schools can be expected to be particularly sensitive and responsive to teacher commitments steaming from professional norms as most principals have the same educational background as their teachers, and in many cases have a long history of being a teacher previous to their managerial position. In many other public organizations managers do not share their employees' educational background and often have a more general or management related training and background. The dual direction of causality may in this case be the reason why the marginal effects of principals' goal prioritization on teachers' goal commitment were not significant, however, the issue cannot be settled here, as the analyses rely on cross-sectional data. The warrant of further studies of the *interaction effect* of goal conflict is thus particularly interesting and necessary. On this background future studies are encouraged to use differently designed studies to further explore this issue. Goal commitment, as defined here, expresses values of the individuals, which are built up over a long time and are thus difficult to manipulate in an experimental set-up. A way to better approach the question of causality could thus be to obtain panel data over time to study how differences over time are interrelated.

In immediate continuation hereof, this study should be considered in view of certain issues and limitations. First of all, a main strength of this paper is the *multilevel data structure*, which provides an unusual opportunity for combining measures of managers' goal prioritization, goal conflict and employees' goal commitment. However, the analyses rely on *cross-sectional survey data*, which besides limiting the opportunities for causal inference as mentioned above, also limits further investigations of the specific mechanisms of the association between principals' goal priorities, goal conflict and teachers' goal commitment. Moreover, conducting similar studies among other occupations and areas of the public sector could test the wider applicability of the findings, beyond the area of secondary education. Especially studies on public employees with weak professional norms would, in the light of the previous discussion, enhance our knowledge in the field. Danish secondary schools are rather similar to for example the American high schools though (Christensen & Pallesen, 2009), why the findings of this study are also considered to have some broader international relevance within the education area.

Secondly, *measures* of goal commitment vary greatly within the literature (Klein, 2001) and the measure used here developed by Meyer and Herscovitch (2001), is rather new compared to the long tradition of the field. Meyer and Herscovitch's items for measuring commitment to goals are however developed on the basis Meyer and Allan's items for measuring commitment to the organization, which are one the most validated scales within the commitment literature (Klein et al., 2012). Furthermore, commitment is here measured using *both* normative commitment and affective commitment items, and together they are theorized to measure an individual's *goal* commitment. This paper, in other words, do not distinguish between these two dimensions, but treat them as one. The factor analysis turns out highly satisfactory and supports this approach, but the reader should be aware of the disparities between this measurement of goal commitment and those seen elsewhere.

Finally, it should be mentioned that the amount of *variance explained* by the presented models is rather low (R2 in Table 3, Model 4 is 0.1343) although a number of control variables have been included in the models. This is not uncommon in similar studies, but it does reflect that relevant variables to the relationship between principals' goal prioritization, goal conflict and employees' goal commitment have been left out of the analyses.

Nevertheless, this article provides new knowledge on the effects of intra-individual goal conflicts in the public sector as well as interesting insights into the *conditions* for reciprocal effects between managers and employees in a public context. If the aim is to increase public employees' goal commitment through goal setting initiatives public managers should be aware of whether there are potential barriers of goal conflict to overcome. This study shows that goal conflicts may be an important context factor for public mangers to consider when designing public personnel policies, and indicates that integrating the organization's strategic goal practices with values that derive from employees' affective and normative values could be the way forward.

REFERENCES

Angle, H. L. and Perry, J. L. (1981): "An empirical assessment of organizational commitment and organizational effectiveness", *Administrative Science Quarterly*, 26:1-14

Brewer, G. A., and S. C. Selden (2000): "Why elephants gallop: Assessing and predicting organizational performance in federal agencies", *Journal of Public Administration Research and Theory*, 10(4): 685-711

Cyert, R. M. and J. G. March (1963). *A Behavioral Theory of the Firm.* Upper Saddle River, NJ: Prentice Hall

Dunham, R. B., Grube, J. A. and Castenada, M. B. (1994): "Organizational commitment: the utility of an integrative definition", *Journal of Applied Psychology*, 79: 370-380

Erez, M., Earley, P. C., & Huhn, C. L. (1985): "The impact of participation on goal acceptance and performance: A two-step model", *Academy of Management Journal*, 28: 50-66

Freidson, E. (2001) *Professionalism: The Third Logic.* London: Polity.

Hackett, R. D., Bycio, P. and Hausdorf, P. A. (1994): "Further assessments of Meyer and Allen's (1991) three-model component model of organizational commitment", *Journal of Applied Psychology*, 79: 15-23

Katz, D. & Kahn, R. L. (1978). *The social psychology of organizations.* New York Wiley

Klein, T. E. Becker, and J. P. Meyer (2009). *Commitment in organizations: Accumulated* wisdom and new directions. New York: Routledge/Taylor and Francis

Klein, H. J., Wesson, M. J., Hollenbeck, J. R., & Alge, B. J. (1999): "Goal commitment and the goal-setting process: Conceptual clarification and empirical synthesis", *Journal of Applied Psychology*, 84: 885–896

Klein, H. J., Molloy, J. C., and Cooper, J. T. (2009): "Conceptual foundations: Construct definitions and theoretical representations of workplace commitments". In H. J. Klein, T. E. Becker, and J. P. Meyer (Eds.), *Commitment in organizations: Accumulated wisdom and new directions*: 3–36. New York: Routledge/Taylor and Francis

Latham, G. P., Borgogni, L., and Pettita, L. (2008): "Goal Setting and performance Management in the Public Sector", *International Public Management Journal*, 11(4): 385-403

Locke, E. A., Latham, G. P. & Erez, M. (1988): "The determinants of Goal Commitment", *The Academy of Management Review*, 13(1): 23-39

Locke, E.A., and Latham, G.P. (1990). *A theory of goal setting and task performance.* Englewood Cliffs, NJ: Prentice-Hall.

Locke, E. A., & Latham, G. P. (2002): "Building a practically useful theory of goal setting and task motivation: A 35-year odyssey", *American Psychologist*, 57: 705–717

Locke, E. A., Smith, K. G., Erez, M., Chan, D. & Schaffer, A. (1994): "The Effects of Intra-individual Goal Conflict on Performance", *Journal of Management*, 20(1): 67-91

Meier, K. J. (1987). *Politics and the bureaucracy: Policymaking in the fourth branch of government.* 2d ed. Monterey, CA: Brooks/Cole Publishing Company

Meyer, J. P. (2009). "Commitment in a changing world of work" in H. J. Klein, T. E. Becker, & J. P. Meyer (Eds.), *Commitment in organizations: Accumulated wisdom and new directions*: 37–68. New York: Routledge/Taylor and Francis

Meyer, J. P., and Allen, N. J. (1997). *Commitment in the workplace: Theory, research, and application.* Thousand Oaks, CA: Sage

Meyer, J. P., and Herscovitch, L. (2001): "Commitment in the workplace: Toward a general model", *Human Resource Management Review*, 11: 299–326

Meyer, J. P.,Allen, N. J.,and Smith, C. A.(1993):"Commitments to organizations and occupations: Extension and test of a three component conceptualization".*Journal of Applied Psychology*, 78:538–551

Meyer, J. P., Stanley, D. J., Herscovitch, L., and Topolnytsky, L. (2002): "Affective, continuance, and normative commitment to the organization: A meta-analysis of antecedents, correlates, and consequences", *Journal of Vocational Behavior*, 61: 20–52

Mintzberg, H (1983). *Power In And Around Organizations*. Englewood, NJ Prentice Hall

Pandey, S. K. and Wright, B. E. (2006): "Connecting the dots in public management: Political environment, organizational goal ambiguity and the public manager's role ambiguity", *Journal of Public Administration Research and Theory*, 16(4): 511-532

Paarlberg, L. E. and J. E. Perry (2007): "Values Management Aligning Employee Values and Organization Goals", *The American Review of public Administration*, 37(4): 387-408

Perry, J. L., Mesch, D. and L. Paarlberg (2006): "Motivating Employees in a New Governance Era:

The Performance Paradigm Revisited", *Public Administration Review*, 66(4): 505–14

Perry, J. L., and L. W. Porter (1982): "Factors affecting the context for motivation in public organizations", *Academy of Management Review*, 7(1): 89–98

Rainey, H. G. (2009). *Understanding and Managing Public Organizations*. John Wiley & Sons, 4th edition

Rainey, H.G. and P. Steinbauer (1999): "Galloping Elephants: Developing Elements of a Theory of Effective Government Organizations", *Journal of Public Administration Research and Theory*, 9(1): 1–3

Roberts, J. and M. Dietrich (1999): "Conceptualizing Professionalism: Why Economics Needs Sociology", *American Journal of Economics & Sociology*, 58: 977-998

Stazyk, E. C., Panday, S. K. and B. E. Wright (2011): "Understanding Affective Organizational Commitment: The Importance of Institutional Context", *The American review of Public Administration*, 41: 603-624

Porter, L. W., W. J. Crampon and F. J. Smith (1976): "Organizational Commitment and Managerial Turnover: A Longitudinal Study", *Organizational Behavior and Human Performance*, 15: 87-98

Stevens, J. M., Beyer, J. M., and Trice, H. M. (1978): "Assessing personal, role, and organizational predictors of managerial commitment", *Academy of Management Journal*, 21: 380-396

Vance, R. J. and Colella, A. (1990): "Effect of two types of feedback on goal acceptance and personal goals", *Journal of Applied Psychology*, 75: 68-76

Wilson, J. Q. (1989). *Bureaucracy. What Government Agencies do and Why They do it*. BasicBooks

Winters, D., & Latham, G. (1996): "The effect of learning versus outcome goals on a simple versus a complex task", *Group and Organization Management*, 21: 236–250

Wright, B. E. (2001): "Public Sector Work Motivation: Review of Current Literature and a Revised Conceptual Model", *Journal of Public Administration and Research Theory*, 11(4): 559-86

Wright, B. E. (2004): "The Role of Work Context in Work Motivation: A Public Sector Application of Goal and Social Cognitive Theories", *Journal of Public Administration Research and Theory*, 14(1): 59-78

Wright, B. E. (2007): "Public Service and Motivation: Does Mission Matter?", *Public Administration Review*, 1: 54-64

APPENDIX A

Table A1. Measurement

Variables	Measurement
Managers' goal prioritization Operationalized as principals' prioritization of a high completion rate	*How do you as manager prioritize the following goals? Rank the goals on a scale from 1-7. 1 for the highest prioritized goal and 7 for the least prioritized goal. Every number can only be assigned once. Write 0 if a goal is not a priority.* • ___ *General education* • ___ *College preparation* • ___ *Teachers wellbeing* • ___ *Students wellbeing* • ___ *High academic level* • ___ *Low drop-out rates* • ___ *Avoid budget deficits*
Employees' goal commitment Operationalized as teachers' affective and normative commitment to the goal of a high completion rate	[Affective commitment] *Achieving a high completion rate is as important to me as it is to the school* *I really want to achieve a high completion rate* [Normative commitment] *I feel obliged to do my best to achieve a high completion rate* *I owe it to my school to do my best to achieve a high completion rate* [1X at a 5 point Likert scale from "completely disagree" to "completely agree"]
Goal conflict Operationalized as teacher perceived conflict between the goals of achieving a high completion and a high academic level	*To which degree do you experience a conflict between securing a high academic level and a high completion rate?* [1X at a 10 point scale from 0 (not at all) to 10 (to a very high degree)]

Table A2. Correlation information

	(1)	(2)	(3)	(4)	(5)	(6)	(7)	(8)	(9)	(10)	(11)	(12)	(13)
(1) Goal commitment (t)	1.000												
(2) Goal prioritization (p)	0.017	1.000											
(3) Goal conflict (t)	-0.327***	0.020	1.000										
(4) Interaction, goalprio*goalconf	-0.217***	0.705***	-0.654***	1.000									
Teacher level control variables													
(5) Age	0.076**	-0.041	-0.086**	-0.076**	1.000								
(6) Gender (female=1)	0.047	0.033	0.010	0.018	-0.121***	1.000							
(7) Tenure, current job	0.009	-0.053	-0.059*	-0.066*	0.818***	-0.118***	1.000						
(8) Teaching area (science=1, other=0)	-0.076**	-0.010	0.011	0.004	0.063*	-0.166***	0.035	1.000					
(9) Part time	0.030	0.032	-0.010	0.025	0.097***	0.016	0.073**	0.029	1.000				
School level control variables													
(10) Principal age	0.028	0.103***	-0.028***	0.075**	-0.044	-0.010	-0.057*	-0.020	0.021	1.000			
(11) Principal gender (female=1)	0.023	0.093***	-0.029	0.043	-0.013	-0.031	-0.023	0.010	0.020	-0.094***	1.000		
(12) Principal tenure, current job	-0.008	-0.055*	-0.028	-0.038	-0.032	-0.033	-0.022	0.017	-0.006	0.674***	-0.053***	1.000	
(13) School size (no. of teachers)	-0.038	-0.029	-0.002	-0.056*	-0.018	-0.018	-0.009	0.041	-0.069*	0.098***	0.011	0.0332	1.000

Note Correlations (Pearson's r). (t) employee level, (p) management level
*p < .05; **p < .01; ***p < .001